TH
TITUS
CONCEPT

Money for
My Best and
Highest Good

by **Al Diaz**

TESTIMONIALS

"If you just read this book, nothing will change for you. However, if you not only read but also do the simple exercises that Al presents, you're very likely to change your life in ways you now can barely imagine."

—Charles Burke
author of Command More Luck
www.CharlesBurke.com

"It is a concise guide to success, with practical information, beautifully compressing the laws of success into a few pages."

—Remez Sasson
www.SuccessConsciousness.com

"Titus incorporates several living ideas of Jesus, Mohammad, Buddha and Shakespeare. Fundamentally, each of us is created in the exact likeness of Divinity: absolute clarity. This absolute clarity, the foundation of Mind, cannot be altered by anything although its affect can be eclipsed by fear and intellectualism. Titus is about letting go, a fundamental step to restoring absolute clarity. Only out of absolute clarity of mind can mind experience wealth beyond all understanding."

—Peace of I, Ihaleakala (Dr. Hew Len)
is president of Pleiades, Inc.
and chairman emeritus of the Foundation of I, Inc.

"Would you like a simple approach to using Mind Power to get what you want out of life? How about an approach so simple, it only has 3 steps? This book shows you how to have the freedom to create and attract the abundant, prosperous, wealthy lifestyle that you desire and require—effortlessly!"

—Alan Tutt
http://www.PowerKeysPub.com

"I'm so excited—I'm bouncing up and down. Your book is amazing, simple and so powerful. Shift your perception, your focus, change your internal and external are the best steps ever. I've read many books on affirmation, visualization and all other self improvement techniques, but your suggestions are unique. It's wonderful and again, simple."

—Emmanuel Segui,
Turn Dreams Into Reality
http://www.vision-to-action.com

With Love and Gratitude
I am forever grateful to you Spirit;
that is the Life, the Energy, and
the Power within all of Creation,
thank you for our book
that this is written on,
and that it will continue to bless others
for our best and highest good,
all ways.

THE TITUS CONCEPT

ISBN: 1-933596-68-6 (Paperback)

Published by:

MORGAN · JAMES
THE ENTREPRENEURIAL PUBLISHER™

Morgan James Publishing, LLC
1225 Franklin Ave Ste 325
Garden City, NY 11530-1693
Toll Free 800-485-4943
www.MorganJamesPublishing.com

Habitat
for Humanity®
Peninsula
Building Partner

Cover and Interior Design by:
Michelle Radomski
One to One Creative Services
www.creativeones.net

My wife Gloria
Thank you for being my guardian angel at the beginning of my deliberate journey.

My daughter Vanessa
Thank you for sticking by me through thick and thin for 18+ years.

My mom
Thank you for showing me all the opportunities and blessings.

My family
Thank you for your Love and support.

My Personal Mentors:
Richard Alaniz
Mary Mitchell
Suzan
Isa De Quesada
Jan Barrios
Travis Loriano

Anywhere from a few days, months, years, to decades, your mentoring guided me to where I am at today. Thank You.

The Only Option Master Mind Group:
Annie Anderson
Christina Menear
David Petrie
Mary Tewhey
Paul Simoneau

Our Mission Statement
To enhance Love and Life by sharing our gifts in guiding others to the best and highest good of all, it is The Only Option.

With much gratitude, Thank You all.

By Dr. Joe Vitale

I met Al Diaz outside of LA at a workshop. He and his wife took me to breakfast and dazzled me with the story of how he created this three step system. I listened to him explain the steps and realized he was on to something big.

I'm honored to write the foreword to this little gem. While my own book, *The Attractor Factor,* contains a five step formula for manifesting whatever you want, Al managed to compress the ideas into three steps.

Truth be known, you only need one step. I've spoken about it, written about it, and have articles about it on my site at www.mrfire.com But most people aren't ready for the one step.

Since they aren't, it's a relief to know Al is coming to the rescue with these three steps.

The point of all of this is simple: Life doesn't have to be hard. Make a couple of decisions, choose what you want, and enjoy the adventure.

Expect miracles , Dr. Joe Vitale
Author of way too many books to mention here, including the #1 bestseller *"The Attractor Factor"*

See http://www.MrFire.com

My full name is Alfred Diaz. I am Hispanic, born and raised in California. My parents were a part of a hard working class in Mexico, who migrated to the United States and became hard working middle class in the U.S.

My parents showed my brother and I we needed the "hard work ethic" to have the money for the things we wanted. One of my parents was very materialistic. In order to satisfy that thirst for material goods, the only way was to work more, longer, and harder. There were times throughout our childhood that both my parents worked two jobs. I also must say our education was important and a high priority for them.

My personal spending money came from jobs I had – starting at 9 years old, when I was a paper boy for the local newspaper, and continuing with many different jobs over my childhood and teenage years.

Without going through all of the details of each experience, suffice to say that I accepted most of the experiences of my first 30 years as fact and truth, though I didn't know it at the time. Because of those facts and truths, this is how I functioned and lived for 40+ years. As a result, I wound up with an inflated ego, sought instant gratification, and had low self esteem.

Do you know what those three characteristics added up to? FEAR! But I didn't know it at the time.

With an inflated ego and an instant gratification mindset, I was able to produce or bring things into my life that I wanted or needed (I thought) to get me through another day, another week, another month, or if I was really good, another year. What this gave me was a sense false sense of confidence. Yet I was always looking over my shoulder to see what was coming up next that I needed to deal with. It was a continuing cycle that was constantly being recycled. There were times that I had it all, and yet the struggle would creep back in. That was because the foundation everything was built on was not strong, but soft from an inflated ego and instant gratification. Add to that the low self esteem I had learned and accepted from others which kept replaying internally and externally, and you can see how my life wasn't always the way I wanted it to be.

So I thought, "this is how life is supposed to be." Some of us were here to struggle, and others were lucky and had all the breaks. I was kind of in a weird place; I struggled, yet still had some lucky breaks. It was like someone was still watching over me regardless what I did.

In the mid nineties I became a certified Massage Technician, which began to take the focus away from myself. I focused on others and their well-being. I eventually became an Emergency Medical Technician where I saw the pain and hurt others endured. That taught me to be grateful for what I have. At the turn of the century I learned how to meditate and though I had found a greater degree of inner peace with meditation, I only did it sporadically. You see I was still functioning with a somewhat inflated ego, instant gratification, and low self esteem – just what seemed normal to me all those years.

MY TURNING POINT

One night at the end of August 2002, I was opening my garage door when it suddenly came back down on top of my head and knocked me out for a few seconds. As I was accustomed to functioning on ego I was in denial that I was badly hurt, until I saw a doctor four days later and he told me that I had a severe concussion. I ended up being put on disability for ten weeks, and though I was very limited in my daily functions, it was probably among the best ten week periods of my life.

I knew I needed to heal physically, so that was what I started to do. After a few days of resting, sleeping and watching TV all day long, I became restless and bored. So I started to meditate, sometimes up to five times a day. Not only did that inner peace become stronger, I started to also discover this inner strength which I didn't recognize before. That brought me to a realization that I also needed to heal mentally, emotionally, and spiritually, along with what I was already doing physically.

As I started to work on my whole being, a whole new world began to open up for me, at all levels and in all areas of my life. Over the next few years I searched for answers and the truth of others. I read as many books as I could, had great mentors, went to seminars, and did everything that I could to keep me moving forward in my life.

During this process I began to attract and create the better things in life for myself. But it was hit or miss at best, sometimes two steps forward and one step back, or one step forward and two steps back. Though I was grateful for what I was accomplishing, I just knew it had to be easier.

I was practicing almost everything I had learned, thinking that perhaps I just needed to perfect the technique(s) to create and attract what I wanted in life. Yet something always felt like it was missing, as if there was one more piece to the puzzle. One day after I came home from work, I continued reading a book I had started some time before by Joe Vitale, called *The Attractor Factor*. About twenty minutes into the reading, I started to feel tired and decided to take a little power nap, so I placed the book on my chest. Ten to fifteen minutes into the nap, my body began to shake uncontrollably – almost seizure. I was still asleep, yet I was fully aware of what was going on. I forced my eyes to open and saw the lower part of my body shaking as if it were in a high vibration. This went on for about ten more seconds, and then stopped. Though I was not scared, I was concerned about what this episode meant. With no clear answer from those I asked, I just moved on and forgot about it.

Several weeks later, I began to notice the crystal clarity of things that came to me, and of my understanding of those things. It was the inner knowing; the Truth, of what and how Life is suppose to be like.

Over and over everything was being played out for me, and everything was starting to make sense. It was like everything I had learned through the years was now simultaneously waking up my inner Wisdom. I started to create and attract situations into my Life more often and frequently.

In a flash that I didn't see coming, all the clarity that seemed infinite came rushing at me. That same clarity is what produced the steps called The Titus Concept that are in this book. You know what they are all about? Here it is:

To be empowered so that you can have the Lifestyle you desire and require effortlessly.

Plain and simple. Nothing more, nothing less.

One big difficulty with money techniques is this – every bookstore has dozens of books dealing with the subject. You may feel frustrated if you have tried any of them and found none suited you. At this point, a lot of people just give up. Does this sound familiar?

Despite what has happened before or what you think, feel, smell, taste, and hear about money, your life is about to change! When you finish reading and properly completing the steps in this book, you will feel a powerful shift in your empowerment vibration.

My intention is to guide you to effortlessly create and attract the lifestyle that you desire and require. The steps in this book will enhance your current understanding and knowledge without adding any dogma, religion, practice, sect, philosophy, science, cult, or other restriction into your Life. By the time you have finished this book, you will have skills the other books did not offer. More importantly, you will have awakened your own inner Spirit to be who you really are.

It does not matter whether you are Catholic, Hindu, Atheist, Spiritual, or just you. These steps are very simple. They will bring about the automatic creation and attraction you desire and require, Choose to do the steps in the book and trust your Self then enjoy the Power you have within you.

Through our life experiences, we have become where we are now, either unintentionally or intentionally. Though the number is growing, very few people have consciously and deliberately created their own lives. They just thought "that is how Life is" or "as fate would have it."

After you have finished this book and carefully practiced what it says, you will be guided to your Truth. This is the inner Truth that very few know. This Inner Truth includes the Power to create using the gifts, talents and strengths you had when you were born.

As you become even more the unique and special person that you are, all the best and highest good things that are perfect for you pour into your life.

Your inner Spirit automatically discards what no longer serves you for your best and highest good. Instead of anything being replaced, it just melts away because it is no longer a part of you or the life you desire and require.

There is no hidden agenda. This is very straightforward and to the point. The steps are very simple. They have worked in my life, and in many other lives, successfully. It works. There is great Truth in each of these steps and in the whole process.

As your Life becomes even more effortless in all areas and at all levels, all I ask is that you share this empowerment with others. Do your part to spread it globally so that others may choose to move away from fear and limitations.

Choose to open your Heart and mind to this book. Read the following statement before you read on the rest of the book:

My Heart and mind are open to allow, receive, accept and use all of the contents of this book for my best and highest good, always.

For more than 20 years I have studied hundreds of books, attended almost as many seminars, and listened to an equal number of tape and CD programs. After just one reading, "The Titus Concept: Money, For My Best and Highest Good" reached into my heart and struck a chord that continues to vibrate in everything I do. Like most people, I do what feels good to me, over and over. Each time I read and practice the steps, I feel energized and excited about the positive changes that I am creating in my life and in the lives around me.

Thank you, Al!

—Paul

— Chapter 1 —

THE TITUS CONCEPT

$$1 + 1 + 1 + 1 = 4$$

The formula is logical and rational; it is very simple. It just adds up the way it is supposed to, and we accept it for what it is.

I have read hundreds of books, thousands of articles, have gone to many seminars, had and have great mentors, and learned from countless life experiences. They all have contributed to where I am Now. It's like all of the pieces of the puzzle were slowly being put together. Those puzzle pieces eventually brought me back home to my inner Wisdom. Then, I had a major "aha," a profound moment! The clarity was dropped in my lap. That is what I am going to share with you in this book.

Look around you and understand this. All of Creation, including each of us, is here to live in a natural state of progression... to grow, succeed, and move forward. This includes happiness and well being. The difference between us and the rest of Creation is; we have free will or free choice. We can choose to grow, succeed, and move forward to becoming the fullest and grandest expression of who we are and can be.

You are reading this book because you attracted it into your Life. I have created this book because I know a Truth, a way that will guide you to create the Life you desire and require (not need or want) effortlessly. This is why we have Now connected.

THE FORMULA

Shift the perception, to shift the focus, to change the internal, to change the external.

That is the premise of The Titus Concept and why it works successfully well. The formula is direct, logical and rational. Just like

1+1+1+1=4, it is very simple and adds up the way it should. The words are perfect and powerful, they are all that is required.

The following chapters contain individual insights first, then a Step for you to do with blank journal pages, followed by comments. I strongly suggest you do one step a day in the order it is presented. Put aside about an hour to do each step; a little longer if you feel journaling will support you.

Are you ready to take command of your Life?

Turn the page and let's get started!

TESTIMONIAL

Thanks for your words, as usual, you're one of the most incredibly wise men I've ever had the honor of knowing.

—Donna Neil

– Chapter 2 –

SHIFT THE PERCEPTION

The Past

Go to a mirror, look deep into your eyes (not at your eyes) and say the following:

My Heart and mind are open to allow, receive, accept and use all of the following processes for my best and highest good, always.

Shift the Perception

INSIGHTS

Many words can help in dealing with your past and what resides in your subconscious, or the accepted beliefs you have. The two most common words are Releasing and Healing. Others you may have heard are: realign, change, and transform. There are many ways to release or heal your past, from traditional counseling to the metaphysical. To a varying degree, they each work. What I am going to show you is direct, simple and powerful.

First, you must understand your past so that you can create the success, prosperity, abundance, wealth, and money you desire.

Let's start by dealing with what you already know. Every money experience you have ever had has contributed to the current condition of money in your Life. That includes every big and small event: the good, the bad, and the ugly, every one. This includes the beliefs of our parents, siblings, teachers, friends, churches, and society. To some extent, you accepted these as your beliefs, which then became your Truth. What is your Truth about money? What do you see regarding your money condition? How do you feel about your money condition? That is your current Truth, your beliefs in regards to money, plain and simple. Another way to put it: it is your very own limitation.

Secondly, every cell in your body has a form of intelligence called DNA. Without this intelligence you would not be who you are – a unique human being. Where does DNA come from? Your parents. Where does their DNA come from? Your grandparents. It goes on and on, so you have generations and generations of DNA from the very beginning, the intelligence that you now have within you.

So what does that mean? Lets say your father's mindset was that he was unsuccessful with money in his lifetime, and your grandfather was the same way. All of this same intelligence gets passed on to each successive generation, which includes you.

Most self-help mentors will tell you, to create or manifest in your life, you require one or more of the following: thoughts, words, or action. Others say emotions and feelings are needed to create and manifest.

Let's say you have had an average (whatever that may be) life experience regarding money. Your beliefs, attitude, mindset, and your truth are average regarding money. Now, let us add the fact that all of your prior generations had an average mindset regarding money. What do you think your thoughts, words, and actions are going to be? Wham! How are you going to be rich if your whole past is average in regards to money!? Are you doomed to an average life of money? As I mentioned, there is everything from counseling to the metaphysical to heal and/or release that average condition of money.

But...

What if I can show you a simpler way? What if I can show you an even more direct way? How about a simple step that is also very powerful?

What you will need:

About one hour to your Self with no interruptions, a mirror, a pen and paper to journal if that works for you, and TRUST!

Best-case scenario is this will have the desired effect after the first try. If you are doing this for the fourth time, you are not trusting the process and in your Self.

TESTIMONIAL

Working with Al Diaz has been a remarkable experience! AL showed up in my life through the TAF group at a time when I needed it most. I have NO idea where I would be emotionally, mentally, spiritually or financially without having the opportunity to work one on one with AL through the steps. Prior to beginning the steps with AL, I was feeling very discouraged with programs, with my spiritual life and my financial circumstances. I had just begun to learn about "vibrations" and "energy" but couldn't quite get myself up to the point where I was manifesting and attracting clients, abundance and other things daily, consistently and predictably. I asked God for a mentor, a partner, someone who could help me get to the other side.

To make a long story short, I worked with AL one on one for one week. Having his guidance and support as well as his easy to implement three steps made all the difference in my life. Plus, I love the fact that AL is so certain in what he believes and conveys to others. I don't feel as if his steps are watered down versions of other programs but something real that anyone, including myself could attach onto with confidence that I could have, do and be whatever I wanted, and to TRUST the process. After working with AL, he encouraged me to TRUST God. As an impatient, aggressive person (at times) I wanted and required everything now, and when it didn't happen, I felt God had let me down. I was tired of being on the rollercoaster of "why" "when" and "how." I wanted and required more. The three steps was the solution. Is the solution.

After working with AL on the steps, the following week over $1200 manifested in my business income. The great thing is, I believe the best is yet to come. I cannot wait to own the CD and materials so I can use them daily to reinforce the steps to stay on the path of wholeness, greatness and financial freedom. To our best and highest good always.

Thank you, Al!

—M. Woods, IL

SHIFT THE PERCEPTION
STEP 1

The subject of your focus is everything that deals directly or indirectly with money.

Think for a few minutes on this question – what is your present money condition regarding?

What do you see?

What do you feel?

What do you think?

What do you speak?

What do you do?

Now, think back to everything you can in relation to money that has brought you to your present monetary condition. Remember everything you can – the good, the bad and the ugly – in other words, everything, from the time you were a toddler until the present moment. Take about ten to fifteen minutes. You want to bring everything you can possibly remember to the forefront of your mind.

Done?

Look in the mirror and into your eyes and state these as FACTS, as your TRUTH:

I acknowledge everything that has transpired before this moment regarding my money condition and that I created this condition as it is now.

I forgive this condition, and in this moment I have released forever the pattern in my consciousness that is responsible for this condition.

I acknowledge and am grateful for my current money condition.

I am happy and thankful for all I have and all I have gone through – every real or imagined thought, belief, mental image, perception, action, word, and feeling – has transpired for my best and highest good.

I Now affirm, intend, mandate, command and choose that everything that contributed to my current money condition is now for my best and highest good. And so it is done; this is the only option.

Allow these statements to settle all the way down to your cells, to your atoms, to your soul, for a period of five to ten minutes. Reread it. The goal is for this be the only time you do this step.

What may happen?

Your ego/mind will challenge you in different ways. It doesn't want to lose the power it has over you. Every time it tries to change your thinking to old pathways, with whatever it brings up, just tell yourself it is Now for my best and highest good. From this day forward, this is how you will answer your ego/mind/fear.

JOURNAL

_____

_____

_____

_____

_____

_____

_____

_____

_____

_____

_____

_____

_____

_____

SHIFT THE PERCEPTION
COMMENTS

TRUST this step has worked. Be grateful this step has worked. Be thankful this step has worked. You have Now transformed your past as well as your personal and generations of experiences to Now be for your best and highest good. You have internalized the experiences so that every part of your being, physical, mental, emotional, and spiritual functions from this premise: that all of your past money experience is for your best and highest good.

Want proof?

Here it is: the fact you are reading this paragraph with the desire to recreate your lifestyle and you felt something inside or saw something in your eyes when you did the above step.

Let me tell you what happened with me. My ego/mind/fear started to play with me. It whispered things to me like: this is silly, this is stupid, what if I trust this and it doesn't work, c'mon, what are your family and friends going to think.

I stood my ground, and reassured my Self that all of my past was for my best and highest good. Guess what? My ego/mind/ fear came at me with a vengeance! It tried to confuse me; to convince me that my past of failures is who I am, that what I am today is what I am to be, that you can never change the past! Who are you kidding?

Again, I stood my ground. This action told my ego/mind that it is Now my servant, my tool, and I am the master of that tool. No longer is my ego/mind or fear running my Life. I was now the deliberate conscious creator of my Life. First, I had to take all of my past back and shift it (not change it,) to a new perspective: for my best and highest good.

Now that you have shifted your past, which has shifted your perspective, you will be living and functioning with more positive energy and vibrant Life.

As you sleep tonight, feel the freedom, and be thankful.

— Chapter 3 —

SHIFT THE FOCUS

The Future

Go to a mirror, look deep into your eyes (not at your eyes) and say the following:

My Heart and mind are open to allow, receive, accept and use all of the following processes for my best and highest good, always.

To Shift the Focus

INSIGHTS

Now that you have shifted your past let us concentrate on your future. Now you have a foundation or root in your Life. Everything prior to this moment is for your best and highest good.

You now have the ability to see and feel an even brighter future for your Self. From this point, you will be functioning from that freedom instead of limitations. So dream, dream big! What would make your heart sing? What would bring you to your knees in joyful gratitude?

Why? Because, you deserve it! You deserve the best and highest good! Not just the highest good, but the best and highest good! You would not want anything less for your loved ones, why would the Power of all Creation want anything less for you? If you desire the best for your loved ones, then desire the best for your Self too! Why leave yourself out of the equation?!

Would you like to be even more empowered? From this point forward get rid of the words "want" and "need," and replace them with "desire" and "require," as you request something for your Self. Use these words in your conversations, your thoughts, and especially in your prayers. You are letting God/Spirit/The Universe know your requests. You are coming from your inner knowing foundation of my best and highest good. This is a powerful vibration, an energy that you externalize that causes you to attract the same energy and create from that same energy.

I desired and required a Master Mind Group for this book. I was coming from my best and highest good and I was creating my future for my best and highest good. What I have attracted and created is an amazing group of people! I already know the group is becoming prosperous, abundant, wealthy and rich in their own right because of it. I know I already have, therefore I see my future as BEing even more prosperous, abundant, wealthy, and rich beyond my wildest dreams.

The time is Now, right Now to create your future. Your new perspective of your past automatically helps you to focus on having an even brighter, vibrant, wealthy future.

This is a powerful step, but one that is fun and enjoyable. Be your own powerful and magnificent genie for an hour, you deserve it.

What you will need:

About one hour to your Self uninterrupted, a mirror, a pen and paper to journal if that works for you, and TRUST!

Enjoy this one and have fun with it.

TESTIMONIAL

Dear Al,

The program is very powerful. When I went through the first step I had so MANY gremlins and limiting beliefs come to my awareness. Before I could go through the process of stating these facts as my truth and forgiving the condition I really went through some stuff! So much so I did even not trust my truth and my faith. I am so appreciative this has come into my awareness, because now I can Truly state these facts as my truth and Really mean it when I forgive these thoughts. Wow so much clearing! This is exactly what I need and where I am at right now. I want to acknowledge your intuition, and your ability to serve and heal people. Fantastic. Thanks so much!

Al Diaz introduced me to a process that changed my life! This process is very powerful and yet gentle at the same time. I highly recommend it! I Love It!

Blessings,

—Lori Valencour

TO SHIFT THE FOCUS
STEP 2

What would you do if you had:

- ❏ Ultimate Success?
- ❏ Amazing Prosperity?
- ❏ Extreme Abundance?
- ❏ Phenomenal Wealth?
- ❏ Powerful Riches?
- ❏ Money beyond your wildest dreams?

Visualize, feel, smell, touch, and hear your answers to the above questions. What would your life be like? When you have your answers in place, fully experience the rich details of your life. Enjoy this for several minutes, enjoy the emotions you feel as you have finally achieved so much, all of what you desire and require. Enjoy it thoroughly before you read on.

Done?

Put what you felt and saw above into a snapshot moment of thought, this will be your own per-sonal moment, snapshot, thought. Something that will forever remain within you, that you are Now becoming.

Ready?

Look in the mirror and deep into your eyes and state this as a FACT as your TRUTH:

I Now intend, affirm, mandate and command that I am thankful and enjoying Ultimate Success, Prosperity, Abundance, Wealth and Money for _____ (insert above thought) which is for my best and highest good, and has arrived rapidly, quickly, and in Divine Order. I thank you Spirit (or whichever name you use) that this blessing is already arriving.

You have stated an end result, you have sent the energy to create what your future will be like: for my best and highest good.

What may happen:

Ego/mind/fear may give you doubts to take the shine off of your bright future. Just enthusiastically tell your Self "it is for my best and highest good and so it is Divinely done!"

TESTIMONIAL

Before I heard about Al's steps, I had suffered from depression for over 40 years. In a day, after applying the steps, I could feel my depression ebbing away. Three things that I had been asking for suddenly came to me in less than a week. And all of it happened without effort on my part.

I have a great feeling about my future now – for the first time in my life, I really believe it is limitless. Al's Titus Concept has woken me up to the fact that everything that has happened to me is for my best and highest good. And that has made a world of difference.

—David Petrie, Ontario, Canada

JOURNAL

_____

_____

_____

_____

_____

_____

_____

_____

_____

_____

_____

_____

_____

_____

TO SHIFT THE FOCUS
COMMENTS

This step is exhilarating! This step you get to do over and over. It's not like you get to pick one future and you're finished. You have the opportunity to recreate your future as many times as you desire or require. As your level of Awareness and your inner Power to create grow, you will continually recreate an even more vibrant future, one that is of infinite possibilities.

With this step you have created a goal, a mission, an intention, a vision, a direction, a path to follow. You have internalized something you desire that is for your best and highest good, and created an energy that emanates from you to attract everything that is required for that manifestation.

Here is the best part: no matter how or what comes to pass it is still for your best and highest good, as that is what you said it would be. If it is not exactly what you hoped for, either the Universe knows something you don't, or more growth is still required. It is still another opportunity to move forward in your life in some way.

All three are a blessing that you consciously and deliberately created, not on a whim or chance.

As you use and increase your ability to create, you live the lifestyle that you desire and require, a life that is for your best and highest good. It doesn't get much better than that!

Tonight dream of what was impossible, because it is possible, and be grateful for what is already arriving.

— Chapter 4 —

CHANGE THE INTERNAL

The Present

Go to a mirror, look deep into your eyes (not at your eyes) and say the following:

My Heart and mind are open to allow, receive, accept and use all of the following processes for my best and highest good, always.

To Change the Internal

INSIGHTS

You have shifted your past, and created a brighter and vibrant future. You have Now automatically changed your internal well being. You know where you are coming from, and where you are headed, and it is all for your best and highest good.

Now to make this even more powerful:

When you created your brighter and more vibrant future with the prior step, you did it in that moment of thought, when it all came to you. In that moment that is the seed of creation, your creation. In every waking moment of your life you are creating, it is a constant flow of creation that never stops.

So what to do? From this point on everything you see, everything you do, everything you hear, everything you feel, and everything you taste in every moment is Now for your best and highest good. This is the same for your future moments, they are all for your best and highest good.

What are you doing? You are consciously and deliberately creating each moment for your best and highest good.

Now, how about if we add money (the reason you bought this book) to this with the following step?

What you will need:

About one hour to your Self uninterrupted, a mirror, a pen and paper to journal if that works for you, and TRUST!

TO CHANGE THE INTERNAL
STEP 3

We have now taken care of your past and your future with the prior steps and transformed them for your best and highest good.

While all the steps and the completion order are equally important, this is the most powerful step.

Your most powerful moment is right Now, this moment, your present. This is where you create.

Look in the mirror and deep into your eyes and state this as a FACT as your TRUTH:

Right Now, this moment, I AM Success, I AM Prosperity, I AM Abundance, I AM Wealth, I AM Rich for my best and highest good! Therefore I AM already becoming even more successful, prosperous, abundant, wealthy and richer for my best and highest good. I AM therefore I AM... Thank you your name that this has already arrived.

State the above effortlessly (like a prayer) right before you go to sleep and the moment you wake up, and at least once during the day. More repetitions are better. You are everything stated above, you are therefore you are for your best and highest good, this is the only option.

Want to make it even more powerful?

Add Spirit(or whatever name you use) and say it is for the best and highest good of all. Now you are creating what all, as one, desire and require. This part is up to you.

State the above often, this is Now you, it is Now fact, it is Now TRUTH.

JOURNAL

_____

_____

_____

_____

_____

_____

_____

_____

_____

_____

_____

_____

_____

_____

TO CHANGE THE INTERNAL COMMENTS

You have just empowered your Self to deliberately and consciously create your Life in every moment. You now state facts that are your Truth, in every moment. You were already doing that automatically with your thoughts, words, actions, and feelings. Now you are doing them consciously and for your best and highest good.

As you put more effort into this step, the day will come when automatically everything already is for the best and highest good. Every request, every meeting, every conversation, every meal, every shower, every step you take, everything! You are already living, functioning, emanating the powerful energy of "for my best and highest good" for what you desire and require with success, prosperity, abundance, wealth and money.

It is automatic, because in this moment and in every moment that is what you are.

Remember, everything you see, everything you touch, everything you hear, everything you smell, everything you taste in each moment consciously create it as: "for my best and highest good."

Here is an example:

Twin brothers go to their place of worship. They both have $20 in their pocket, and both do not get paid until that coming Friday. When it is time to tithe, one brother says 'I can't afford to give today, all I have is $20 until Friday,' the other brother says 'I will give $10 because it is for my best and highest good, I can afford it, and I trust will be taken care of.' Look at what each brother is creating! Who is already poor? Who is already rich?

Because you have shifted your perspective and your past, it is much easier for you to deliberately create an abundant, vibrant Life. This is who you Now are.

Start this moment, create Now, do it Now. The next word, the next step, the next thought, the next emotion, just say it 'it's for my best and highest good.' So it is. It is done.

TESTIMONIAL

This is just a brief account of everything that's manifest for me since using the Steps:

As you already know, I've gained a tremendous sense of peace as I shared on the call Wednesday but in addition to that, I've lost 15 pounds since October 7th, "found" $100 I didn't know I had, and every time our family needs something, from gas to groceries to a close parking spot at the store or whatever, it just seems to appear or the money to buy them is suddenly available. We also found our dream house and got approved for the mortgage to buy it and will be closing in the next few weeks. And, probably the biggest thing, I got home in time from my business trip to Phoenix to say goodbye to Grandma before she passed away. That included changing flight plans and all kinds of things that normally would have been extremely difficult and time consuming but it all just flowed together in about 10 minutes. And there's actually been more things, but I'll stop here.

—Annie

— Chapter 5 —

CHANGE THE EXTERNAL

The Creation

Go to a mirror, look deep into your eyes (not at your eyes) and say the following:

My Heart and mind are open to allow, receive, accept and use all of the following processes for my best and highest good, always.

To Change the External

INSIGHTS

At this point you may want to take a day off. Almost everyone I mentored I had them take a day off to rest and let everything that has transpired settle down to their core. I even suggest on this day of rest to look around and see what you notice new and different internally and externally. Either way, let's continue.

If it were possible, I would be with every single person reading this book, to encourage and lead you on to your success, prosperity, abundance, wealth, and money for your best and highest good. Every single person deserves the best and highest good.

Now you have accepted that your past, present, and future is for your best and highest good. Pay attention to what is going on around you, be grateful for what is going on around you, because with this new acceptance, you will see and feel a more vibrant life. This new life helps you create more effortlessly what you desire and attract what you require.

Be patient! Sometimes we want (used that word purposely) something urgently. Perhaps the rent is due, or on a larger scale money needed (used the word purposely) for a business deal. When you are in this type of situation, acknowledge that you created it and you are in a need or want mindset. Reject it and release it. Turn the scenario around and tell your Self this is for my best and highest good, and then absolutely TRUST! Regardless of what your mind says, or what your ego tells you, or what fear comes up with, TRUST! Know that if you have the ability to create where you are now, TRUST you have the ability to RE-CREATE, especially for what you desire and require!

The following step is for encouragement, as if I were with you. Anytime you feel you desire or require a boost, look at this step. I recite it almost every day to keep me going forward; I know it will do the same for you.

You deserve it! It is time. It is your time.

What you will need:

About 15 minutes to your Self uninterrupted, a mirror, a pen and paper to journal if that works for you, and TRUST!

TO CHANGE THE EXTERNAL
BONUS STEP

To help you along and stay on the path for your best and highest good:

Look in the mirror and deep into your eyes and state these as FACTS as your own personal TRUTH:

- I am open to any and all possibilities, and willing to see this current condition differently and letting me see a new, healed and even better perspective.

- I now intend, affirm, command, mandate, accepted, and choose this: I am vigilant internally and externally for the newly visible in each moment for an even more abundant life in everything I deal with, sooo glad to be right here – right now, having even more perfect skilled discernment, and accept and surrender to what is.

- YES! All of this is for my best and highest good.

JOURNAL

_____

_____

_____

_____

_____

_____

_____

_____

_____

_____

_____

_____

_____

_____

_____

TO CHANGE THE EXTERNAL
COMMENTS

Those who have mastered their lives are able to keep their energy pretty even day in and day out. Those of us who are at other levels of self mastery will have our energy fluctuate at varying degrees depending on who we are and where we are at in our lives. This bonus step is to keep your energy up and evenly, to live and function in this manner. Perhaps one day, if we ever meet, we can look into each others eyes and know we have mastered having the energy to effortlessly create what we desire and require for our best and highest good in success, prosperity, abundance, wealth, and money. We would emanate that energy and it would be noticeable all around us.

You know why?

Because we deserve it!

TESTIMONIAL

These steps have changed my life in so many ways. Even though our income was cut in half, we still have enough money to meet all our bills, which is amazing to me because we were barely meeting our obligations with two incomes! My son half-heartedly tried the steps and ended up getting a job that he loves. Two hours later, after being on the job for 8 hours, he was promoted & given a $2.00 per hour raise! Everything that happens in my life is now for my best and highest good, and I believe it! Please don't take my word for how powerful these three simple steps are!!!! Try them yourself and see the amazing difference they will make.

—Mary

— Chapter 6 —

FINAL COMMENTS

Let us say you have transformed (not changed) your past for your best and highest good, as in step one. What have you done by doing that?

Effortlessly you:

- Heal what no longer serves you

- Release what no longer serves you

- Realign your thought process to have an even more vibrant past

Let us say you also have transformed your future for your best and highest good, as in step two. What is that doing?

Effortlessly:

- You set a goal, a vision of what you desire

- You internalize what you truly desire (it has been there all along)

- You externalize to the whole Universe your desire

- All the seen and unseen energies create your future, your Truth, per your intention.

Now let us say you create in every moment for your best and highest good, in the present, when we are the most powerful, as in step three. Guess what?

Effortlessly:

- You are in control of your Life

- You are the creator/master of your Life

- Your mind/ego is your servant, as it should be, not your master

- You are deliberately and consciously creating the Life you desire in every moment

Finally, what if...

Your present, past and future are all BEing for your best and highest good. What will you get?

- Your vibration is for your best and highest good

- Your energy is for your best and highest good

- Your essence is for your best and highest good

- Your Light is for your best and highest good

- Your Love is for your best and highest good

- Your Spirit is for your best and highest good

- Your emotions are for your best and highest good

- Your thoughts are for your best and highest good

- Your spoken word is for your best and highest good

- Your feelings are for your best and highest good

- Everything is for your best and highest good

What do you think will happen then?

The floodgates open. At this point you receive, require, deserve, desire, accept, allow, experience and use all that is for your best and highest good. You know what else? You are racing with Spirit to give away the blessings you are receiving, then it is fun.

BEing exactly who you are, and for your best and highest good, SHOULD NOT be difficult!

Your ego/mind/fear may come back right at you fighting, maybe with fear, doubt, confusion, or with vengeance. Why? Do you think ego wants to lose this power? If you were a master of something and all of a sudden you were told you were now the servant would you jump up and down for joy? Nope!

Always acknowledge what ego says, do not resist it or bury it internally; that just gives it more energy. As you acknowledge what ego tells you, even tell it thank you for looking out for you. Then, tell it this is for my best and highest good, and be the master that you are, and have your mind/ego as your tool, it is here to serve you for the best and highest good. So, take the Power back!

Living and functioning in this Light, your Life will become even more effortless, in all areas, and in all levels. It is an awesome feeling! Perhaps when Jesus walked on water, he did it for our best and highest good. Do you see? It was the only option, anything less wasn't an option! That is how all the masters lived, for the best and highest good of all.

Please understand these steps are to bring about the Awareness that you desire and require, the TRUTH that is already within you. The tears you shed, the butterflies you felt, the power you sensed, even the mixed feelings you had, that is your inner Spirit waking up. The inner Spirit that has been waiting for you to say 'I am ready', so it can guide you to create/attract what you desire. This is called Empowerment. Using these steps, you are on the path of empowering your Self. Nothing can give you the answers you seek because you already have the answers within you.

The best anyone or anything can do is to guide you to the Wisdom within you. When you then tap into that Wisdom, that is when you have those profound or "aha" moments, or as they say the light bulb goes on.

As I indicated before, I have read many books. Every single one contributed to where I am Now. There is one chapter in the book by Joe Vitale in The Attractor Factor that forever changed my Life. In that chapter the first sentence reads 'Will you join me in transforming the world?' That brought a twinge in my Heart. In that same chapter he introduced an experiment that runs for 30 days at a time, and the success is determined by the end result. I did three experiments in a row, and they all came to pass. Everything I have read, everything I had been told prior to this was all coming clear. It was like all the pieces of the puzzle were being put together and fitting perfectly. The clarity I Now have transformed me from a student of success to BEing success as an end result. I also understood that the world is required to know this clarity, and desired it to be done simplistically so that everyone can grasp it.

That is how this book came about.

Everything I have been through has brought me to this point in time, this opportunity, this blessing of my accelerating Self Awareness, my inner Wisdom, and the absolute unconditional Love for my Self to create these steps.

With these steps I have greatly simplified the Empowerment process to happen as quickly as possible, because I deserve (as well as you) the best and highest good. Why would we want anything less, or why would the Creator of all creation want anything less for us? Understand that we have placed all limitations on ourselves (I no longer do). Well, enough is enough, this is the time, our time, that everything is for our best and highest good, and doing so with simplicity, and with a powerful shift.

Just like all of Creation, YOU are here to grow and succeed! The Power of all Creation desires for you to grow and succeed. Look around you, what do you see? Even those less fortunate are doing what they can to survive. That is our innate desire. But we must choose to move forward, we must desire and require to move forward. In this book I have given you a simple and effortless way to do it. There is nothing to replace, what this book does is enhances what you already know. Whatever else that you no longer desire or require just melts away, because it is no longer a part of you or who you are. When you are living and functioning for 'my best and highest good' that is what you will attract, and that is what you create from, nothing else can come from it, it is that simple. Guess where the most powerful support will come from? From the Power/Spirit of all Creation, the same Power that you have within YOU! When the Power of all and the same Power that is within you is working hand in hand or in congruence for the best and highest good for you to grow and succeed in money, prosperity, abundance, and wealth, then your Life becomes even more effortless. It is that simple, it is that effortless.

As you live and function this way, you have an inner knowing, so that whatever comes your way you are empowered to keep moving forward. Understand and know this: YOU deserve the best and highest good, so allow it, receive it, accept it, and utilize it. Express it to your Self daily; make it an automatic loop in your conscious and subconscious mind. To make it even more concrete within you, share this with others, share your new found wealth, share your empowerment and empower others, because it is time. It is OUR time. The time is Now to have changed ourselves to change the world for OUR best and highest good, always. It is the only option.

These steps are here to light the fire of the inner Spirit that is within each of us, the Spirit that is the Power of all creation, the Spirit that flows through all Creation, the Spirit that connects us all, the Spirit we emanated from.

Shift the Perception, to Shift the Focus, to Change the Internal, to Change the External.

Then it will be all yours...

Al

TESTIMONIAL

I have always been interested in reading any material on improving your finances, but this is the first time I actually found what I was looking for. These three easy steps have put my financial life in perspective. I am so grateful to understand that although I have made mistakes, they brought me to the point I am now. I am ready to receive. I know that everything I do is for my best and highest good and the good of all. My life has changed almost over night. There is tremendous power and confidence that comes from releasing the past and letting the Universe guide you to your true path and purpose, while blessing you beyond your wildest dreams. I look forward with anticipation to each new day and the abundance and love it brings!!! It is the only option!!!!

For our best and highest good!!!

—Christina M., Pinehurst, NC
www.intuitiveassets.com

— Chapter 7 —

WHAT IS COMING

As you understand this process, and the simplicity of having a lifestyle that is effortless. You will start to notice that this process can be applied to all areas and all levels of your Life. So the more you function in this manner, the more it automatically becomes part of who you are. It is here to Empower you, to enhance the inner Truth within you so that you may become the grandest and fullest expression of who you are effortlessly.

Be ready, as your spirit grows, so does your success, prosperity, abundance, wealth, and riches beyond your wildest dreams. The great part is everything you achieve and have is your very own definition of all of the above, nobody else's.

Ride the wave of the best and highest good.

Next: The Titus Concept: Relationships, For My Best and Highest Good – Fall 2006

RU Ready?

TESTIMONIAL

Ever since I tried the technique, my life has completely changed for the better in every way. My income has gone up by $500 a month, and it looks like it will probably be going up more. I came into $2400 and managed to get all my Christmas shopping... and then some... done. I passed my driver's license!!!! In Ontario Canada, it takes 2 years in a graduated program to become a licensed driver... I made it through in 39 days!!! My brother bought me a mini-van and paid the insurance on it for the year. My ex-husband has put his foot in it and is on his permanent way out of mine and the children's lives!... and the big one... after leaving my cruelly abusive husband, I couldn't figure out how I was ever going to afford to pay for my children's sports, especially my daughter's figure skating... well, the money just is, and my daughter started figure skating today. I feel like I'm in the middle of a dream that just keeps on getting better and better and better.

I made a sign, by hand, that says "For Our Best and Highest Good." It is hanging on the wall where it is the last thing I see at night and the first thing I see every morning. Since hanging the sign there, the power of this technique has taken hold and is kicking in even stronger!!! I fall asleep with this mantra in my head, and I wake up to it.

Thank you so much Al, you've brought so much positive into my life with this astounding technique!

For Our Best and Highest Good!

—Donna Neil

Chapter 8

RESOURCES I RECOMMEND

Please note and understand: You already have all the answers internally. You have all the Wisdom you desire and require within you. All you have to do is tap into it. The best anyone or anything can do is to guide you. Anyone who says they have the answers is misleading you to a Life of up and down cycles and challenges. But those who say they are here to guide you to your inner Truth that already exists within you, where you will find all of your answers you will live a Life that becomes even more effortless.

The following resources are only a few of the many, many that I have studied. I have chosen these to pass on to you because since 2003 these have had a powerful impact on me to guide me to my inner Wisdom.

Wherever you get your guidance from, listen to your Heart, feel from your Heart. When something comes to you and you feel a twinge in your Heart keep it because it's waking up something inside you. At the other end if anything just doesn't feel good just discard it and tell your Self 'next,' to ready your Self for your next guidance.

If Life Is A Game, These Are The Rules
By Cherie Carter-Scott

The Power of Now
By Eckhart Tolle

The Power of Intention
By Dr. Wayne W. Dyer

Your Best Life Now
By Joel Osteen

The Attractor Factor
By Joe Vitale

The One Minute Millionare
By Mark Victor Hansen & Robert G. Allen

The Joy Book, And Also The God Book
By Prem Raja Baba

Imagine 21 Fast Track to Change
Lou Tice, The Pacific Institute

The Only Option Master Mind Group
www.theonlyoption.net

If you'd like to write to us, you may do so by sending an email to info@theonlyoption.net

Look for more great materials from us, The Only Option Master Mind Group, throughout 2006.

There is a lot of guidance in these resources; each one may bring you closer to your inner Truth.

— Chapter 9 —

TROUBLESHOOT

Just in case the model is slow to respond to the above transformation, please do the following.

Look in a mirror and deeply into your eyes and verbally say:

Your first name, I honor who you are and what you are, I honor your spirit, love, energy, and light.

Your first name, I love you and I think you are special, what can I do right Now to make you happier?

The above is best done right before you go to sleep, and soon after you wake up.

When you are in public and you see your reflection just silently tell your Self: I love you and I honor you. Even give your Self a wink ;) as you tell your Self, like you have a secret that the rest of the world doesn't know.

PS The model is you!

Chapter 10

BONUS CHAPTER

The Power of Intention, Master Mind, and Purpose for **The Best and Highest Good, for All**

In previous chapters, I indicated when you live your Life for the best and highest good for your Self, the floodgates open and all the blessings start pouring into your Life. Granted, some of the blessings may not be what you 'wanted'. Just remember, what you do get is always for your best and highest good, as that is what you requested, that is what you desired, and that is what you required.

When all this clarity came rushing to me, I took a big gamble and introduced these steps that I didn't have a name for yet to twenty complete strangers that I knew very little about. I was looking for their feedback to assure I was functioning in a reality that made sense and actually worked. Sixteen of the twenty came back with positive feedback; most of the sixteen used the word 'powerful' to describe the steps.

My Purpose in Life up to this point was to enhance Love and Life. After the feedback and confirmation of the steps, I boosted my Purpose by adding an intention that everyone should be empowered to have the freedom in creating and attracting a Lifestyle for their best and highest good effortlessly.

So, now I knew my Purpose and I had my Intention to go along with it. Now, how do I get it out to the world? I remembered two words I had previously learned: Master Mind.

It is a recognized fact that when several people brainstorm and work on a project together, there are more breakthroughs and unique perspectives available than if just one person was working on it. Our mastermind group is simply a group of people divinely bonded together to work on a common objective, the Titus Concept. There is such power and energy in our group; collectively, we continue to accomplish things that amaze us! The book, steps, and Master Mind group have all played a part in changing the way I approach life at a soul level. How much my thinking had been transformed became clear to me the night my husband had a heart attack. I set the intention that this situation would be for the best and highest good of all concerned and TRUSTED everything would work to that end. After a two-day stay in the hospital as well as three stents placed in his heart, he was back to work in 2 weeks – even the doctors couldn't believe how quickly he improved. What it comes down to is this: Allow yourself to trust, know EVERYTHING that occurs is for the best and highest good, and be truly grateful for all that comes your way. Let the magic begin!

—Mary Tewhey

You see, I had to listen to my Heart and TRUST everything was for my best and highest good, because I went ahead and proposed to these same twenty complete strangers what I felt was a great opportunity for their support in getting these steps out the world. Guess what?! I received a collection of replies with testimonials and support. The Joy I felt was overwhelming and held me in amazement. People who barely knew me were willing to help me! The support, insights, gifts, talents, and strengths came quickly from all the members of the group. We quickly had our first conference call in early October, literally days after the Master Mind group was formed.

The definition of a "Master Mind" as defined by Napoleon Hill in Think and Grow Rich is "Coordination of knowledge and effort, in a spirit of harmony, between two or more people, for the attainment of a definite purpose." This is a meeting of the minds so to speak, but it is so much more. I have an additional definition by Dr. Joe Vitale and Pat O'Bryan from the Law of Success Workbook, a "Master Mind" may be created through the bringing together, in a spirit of perfect harmony, two or more minds. No group of minds can be blended into a Master Mind if one of the individuals of that group possesses a negative mind. The negative and positive minds will not blend in the sense here described as a Master Mind.

When two or more people harmonize their minds and produce the effect known as a "Master Mind," each person in the group becomes vested with the power to contact and gather knowledge through the subconscious minds of all the other members of the group. This power becomes immediately noticeable. The minds of those participating in the "Master Mind" become as magnets, attracting ideas and thought stimuli from no one knows where!

Power is organized knowledge, expressed through intelligent effort."

To me, this is what we have experienced with "The Only Option" Master Mind group. We had all done the steps, set an Intention and were guided together. Originally, we were 9 or 10 in number, but as this says the minds must all be positive to work. We ended up with 6. If you look at it, 6 is the perfect number, and if you add Spirit we have 7, like the letter G as in Gratitude. From the moment we became six minds, the power of Purpose and Intention kicked in. We were constantly awed by the energy, and dynamic creative force that flowed through the group.

Individuals rose to challenges, pushed beyond their normal comfort zone effortlessly and joyfully. The ideas and solutions to every step were beyond what anyone of us could imagine. The Power of the Master Mind is not just that you have 6 minds working as one, but rather you hundredfold your resources, and you enlist the higher power of the Universe to assist you and guide you. The project was and is now Spirit driven for the Best and Highest Good of All! It seems to grow and increase in scope and energy with each day and each new idea. The overflow of blessings extends into each of our lives as well. A short three months ago we were total strangers, brought together by our common thirst for answers. We have accomplished an

*amazing amount of work through the Power of
Intention, the Power of Focus and Purpose and
the amazing Power of the "Master Mind."*

—Christina Menear

A few weeks after the first conference call, the
book you are Now reading 'The Titus Concept:
Money, for My Best and Highest Good" was
created and completed. We continued to quickly
move forward as opportunities presented
themselves. We functioned as One, for the best
and highest good of all. On November 25th,
2006 the website www.theonlyoption.net was
introduced to the world, containing the e-book
version you are now reading. Everything was
done within two months! Nothing was prede-
termined! It all came to pass swiftly and quickly.
Why? It was for OUR best and highest good. It
was The Only Option.

*When Al asked us to write about our experience,
I sat down with no idea what I should write
because being a part of this MasterMind Group
and working with Al on the steps provided in*

The Titus Concept has changed my life significantly in many ways. In order to convey to you how important this is, how awesome this is, let me first tell you about myself and a couple of events that have happened in my life recently. Unfortunately, I can't write about this in a few sentences – it's much too powerful for that – so I hope you'll stick with me here...

My family is a very large and close-knit one. This year, we lost both my maternal grandparents a few months apart. My grandfather was diagnosed with liver cancer in February and passed away 8 weeks later. Our family was devastated. I was stressed out and had gained weight. Everything in my life became a burden.

And then in September, my grandma who had suffered a stroke in 1997 began to rapidly decline and passed away in October. But this time, though the loss of my grandma was no less significant, I handled it in a much different way and instead of gaining weight, I actually lost weight and felt at peace. The difference was The Titus Concept.

This was only the beginning. See, I've owned my own business for a long time but still had to work for someone else in order to make ends meet. I always felt as though I was running around like the proverbial chicken with my head cut off. Now, with the Titus Concept and the Power of the Mastermind Group, I'm getting closer to being able to quit my "job" and do what I want to do full time. I have much less stress, I have clarity in most areas of my life and my relationships are growing stronger. It's simply amazing how rapidly things advance in ones life when things are in harmony. And part of the beauty and magnificence of the Titus Concept is that you can do the steps as often as you feel you need to.

Please do not hesitate to contact us if you'd like support as you progress on your journey. We're all here to help support you! We'd love to see you join our Yahoo! Group.

Blessings,
Annie (LeAnne) Anderson

Yes, it is The Only Option. Why would anyone desire anything less than the best and highest good? The Power of Purpose, the Power of Intention, the Power of the Master Mind all focused on what is the best and highest good for all, moves the Power of all Creation to that end result, and that is what we all desired and required. This is why you are reading my book, that same Power has Now connected us.

I "met" Al via our active participation in The Attractor Factor community. We quickly discovered that, though we live on different coasts, we have multiple things in common. Central to those commonalities is the core knowing that we each have special knowledge to share. We know that we can offer people the tools to improve their own life and the lives of those around them.

When Al asked me to be part of The Only Option Master Mind group, I felt the energy of possibility. For years, I have read about the magic that happens when people with common beliefs come together for a higher purpose.

If this group shared some of the same beliefs that Al and I share, the power and potential would be incredible.

As it has turned out, the synchronicity in this Master Mind group is all I had hoped to find and much, much more. Not only do Al and I share this or very similar beliefs, every member of The Only Option does as well. Our common belief is so strong that we were able, in a single conference call, to agree on a group mission statement that still rings true down to my cells: "Enhancing love and life by sharing our gifts in guiding others to the best and highest good of all, the only option."

With the group's mission in alignment with my personal mission, it has been like having a close group of friends who get what I am about. The emails we share daily and the weekly conference calls go a long way in helping me stay on course with my personal work as well as the projects we share.

Each member of our group is incredible as an individual. I am amazed and honored to know them separately and as a group. It has never been more true than in our group that "one plus one equals 11." The synergy is absolutely amazing, far beyond what I could have predicted. My imagination is far less limited thanks to these life changers. Not in a Master Mind group? Read Napolean Hill's "Think and Grow Rich" then join/create one. It really is for your Best and Highest Good.

Then there is this incredible book. Reading through the draft, I felt a shift in my energy. Could it really be this easy? I went through the book again and took my time reading through and working through each step. With all that I have learned, I quickly accepted responsibility for being where I am in my life. I also know that all that has happened and is happening has made me who I am and is clearly for my Best and Highest good.

Yes, the steps are truly effortless but the process is less easy for me than it seemed after my first time through. It is taking repetition to peal back the many layers of beliefs that that I have pasted on for half a century. For me, that means working through the steps multiple times to discover what I may have missed on previous times. Each time, new lights are going on and staying on. Every time I do the steps, new circuits are firing. New clarity opens up. I feel what a flower must feel as it unfolds to bloom and fulfill its destiny.

My relationship with money was the initial motivation for working through the steps, in my experience that is only the tip of the mountain of mind-expanding spiritual experiences that these steps and the Titus Concept are unfolding. I clearly see an ever-expanding community of people sharing their discoveries and experiences and learning from each other.

I am already in the beginnings of that community. Without closing my eyes, I see more support tools rolling out as the community grows and shares. I feel the planetary shift in consciousness to a mindset that releases fear. I hear every member of our community openly saying words that are for the Best and Highest good of all of us. I smell the fresh sweet fragrance of new life and of lives renewed. I taste the crystal clean flavor or pure intention. I know everything is for the Best and Highest good of all.

Imagine the world when we reach the point of having enough people who are living for the Best AND Highest Good of All of us. Got it? Need to do the steps again?

—Paul Simoneau

Using your own unique gifts, strengths, and talents you have the same ability for the same type of success and more. There is no luck involved. What do you desire? What do you require? Make that choice Now! Live the Life of your dreams. Now is the time, yesterday is gone and tomorrow is yet to come. Why wait another moment?

Would you like a blessing? You got it! We already know The Titus Concept is becoming a global understanding. As I write this in mid December, the e-book had already been purchased in Asia, Australia, Europe, and across North America including Canada. This is only after a few weeks of availability. Here is the blessing: we have formed a community that is free to join of people just like you who are just beginning the process, and those who have mastered the process. I encourage you to join through our website at www.theonlyoption.net.

Do you require more encouragement? How about another blessing that is outrageous?! Go to our website www.Morgan-James.com/titus and get the audio version of the steps on CD FREE of charge! All you have to do is pay a few dollars for shipping and handling.

That is how very much we believe in this process. It shows why David Petrie, another member of the Master Mind, created the www.theonlyoption.net website on his own time. We believe in the process called The Titus Concept. You are reading the book because it is your time, you deserve it, effortlessly.

To OUR best and highest good, always. It is The Only Option.

Al Diaz

P.S. Here is a final thought that was given to me and I would like to pass on to you:

THE IMPORTANCE OF MASTERMINDING

Masterminding occurs when two or more individuals get together in the spirit of cooperative harmony to accomplish some goal, activity or result. Almost all of the great accomplishments and miraculous achievements of history were brought about through the power of this principle.

Jesus used masterminding. He personally selected twelve men and told them, "Follow me." They did, and the world has never been the same. Orville and Wilbur Wright did what was said to be impossible by building and flying the first airplane. Andrew Carnegie aggregated a team around him and built the world's biggest steel manufacturing company. Carnegie went on to become the first great philanthropist – funding over three thousand public libraries throughout the world. Likewise, Bill Gates and Paul Allen started Microsoft and became two of the richest men of all time and are now becoming two of the world's greatest living philanthropists.

Thomas Edison, the world's greatest inventor, had many mastermind partners. Edison's most famous mastermind partner was Henry Ford. When Mr. Edison's New Jersey laboratory burnt to the ground, Mr. Ford arrived the next morning and handed Edison a check for $750,000 and encouraged him to "Start building again." Ford would not accept interest on his loan; he just wanted his best friend to get back to work.

Great success is only achieved as the result of great teamwork. Team is an acronym that means Together Everyone Achieves More. Can you think of other great teams? Walt Disney and his brother Roy. Michael Jordan and Phil Jackson. Steven Spielberg and George Lucas. Jack Canfield and Mark Victor Hansen combined, activated and accentuated each others' talent to create the phenomenally successful Chicken Soup for the Soul series which has sold more than eighty million books worldwide with 29 best selling licensed products including calendars, greeting cards and games.

Your greatness lies in your ability to attract to yourself a great team. Begin your team now – whether you are ready or not. Start with people you know. Search out a mastermind associate who you trust, respect and admire – someone who wants to work with you to accomplish great things and who has core competencies that are strong where you are weak, and vice versa. As you grow and develop, add more team members and/or form new teams.

"One plus one, doesn't equal two. It becomes the power of eleven."

—Mark Victor Hansen

Something magic happens when two or more people combine their single dream to form a dream team.

Read this book again, at the very least the steps. Do them to increase even more the end results you desire and require for your best and highest good. Let us know your successes and insights on our website www.theonlyoption.net, it will solidify your growth process even more.

This is not The End, this is The Beginning. Contact us, it is worth the blessings.

JOURNAL

_____

_____

_____

_____

_____

_____

_____

_____

_____

_____

_____

_____

_____

_____

_____

JOURNAL

_____

_____

_____

_____

_____

_____

_____

_____

_____

_____

_____

_____

_____

Printed in the United States
50775LVS00001B/259-264

9 781933 596686